W9-DGF-647

202578

GRAPHIC HISTORIES
THE CALIFORNIA GOLD RUSH

STORY:
ELIZABETH HUDSON-GOFF AND DALE ANDERSON

ILLUSTRATIONS:
GUUS FLOOR

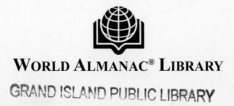

WORLD ALMANAC® LIBRARY

LONG BEFORE THE GOLD RUSH, NATIVE AMERICANS LIVED ON THE LAND THAT IS NOW CALIFORNIA. THEY LIVED BY FARMING AND HUNTING.

BUT IN 1769, THE SPANISH EMPIRE TOOK OVER CALIFORNIA. SPANISH RULERS WANTED TO OWN THE LAND AND CONTROL THE NATIVE PEOPLE WHO LIVED THERE.

THE SPANIARDS KILLED MANY OF THE INDIANS AND FORCED OTHERS TO BE SLAVES.

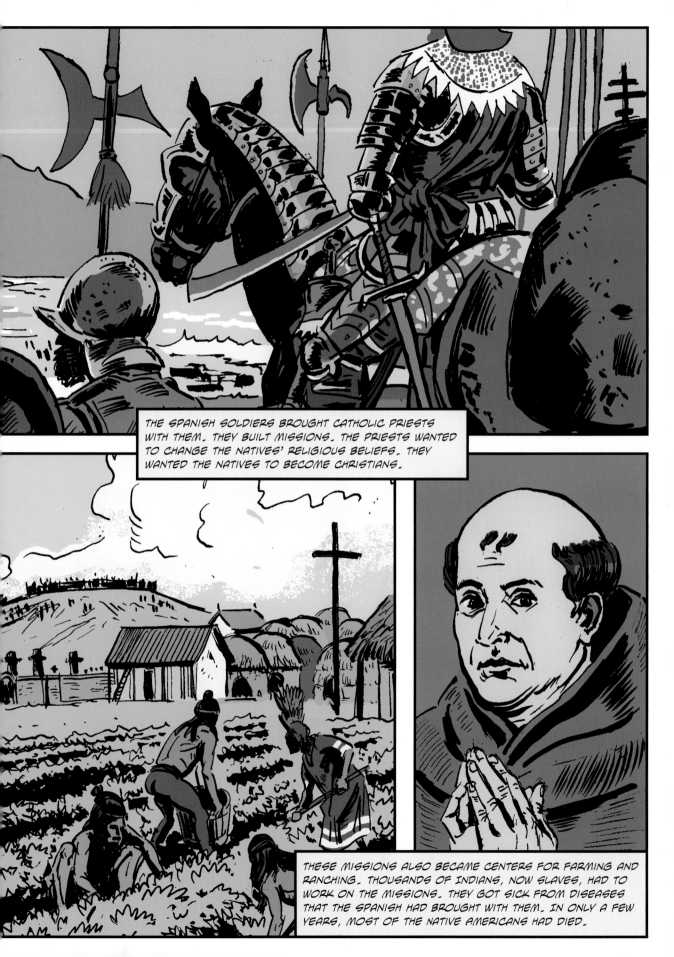

THE SPANISH SOLDIERS BROUGHT CATHOLIC PRIESTS WITH THEM. THEY BUILT MISSIONS. THE PRIESTS WANTED TO CHANGE THE NATIVES' RELIGIOUS BELIEFS. THEY WANTED THE NATIVES TO BECOME CHRISTIANS.

THESE MISSIONS ALSO BECAME CENTERS FOR FARMING AND RANCHING. THOUSANDS OF INDIANS, NOW SLAVES, HAD TO WORK ON THE MISSIONS. THEY GOT SICK FROM DISEASES THAT THE SPANISH HAD BROUGHT WITH THEM. IN ONLY A FEW YEARS, MOST OF THE NATIVE AMERICANS HAD DIED.

IN 1821, THE PEOPLE IN MEXICO
REVOLTED AGAINST SPAIN. THEY
FOUNDED THE REPUBLIC OF MEXICO.
FOR THE NEXT 25 YEARS, CALIFORNIA
AND OTHER AREAS THAT ARE NOW
PART OF THE U.S SOUTHWEST
BELONGED TO MEXICO.

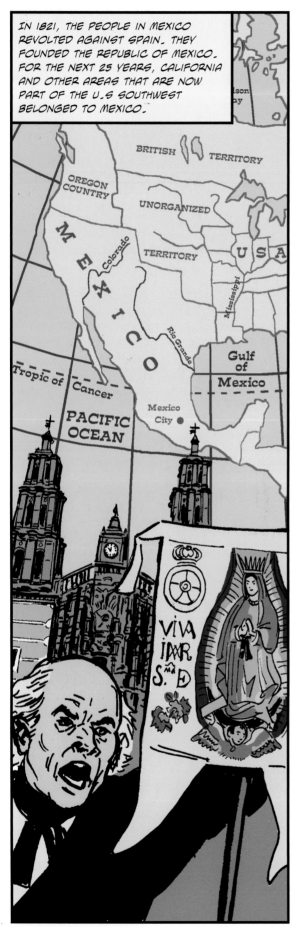

BUT THE UNITED STATES OF AMERICA WANTED CALIFORNIA. AMERICANS BELIEVED IT WAS THEIR DESTINY TO RULE THE CONTINENT. IN 1846, MEXICO AND THE UNITED STATES WENT TO WAR.

A SMALL GROUP OF AMERICANS WHO LIVED IN CALIFORNIA ALSO PROTESTED BEING UNDER THE RULE OF ANOTHER COUNTRY. THEY WANTED TO MAKE CALIFORNIA A SEPARATE COUNTRY CALLED THE CALIFORNIA REPUBLIC. IN 1846, THEY RAISED A FLAG WITH A BEAR ON IT. THE "BEAR FLAG REVOLT" ENDED WHEN THE U.S. NAVY ARRIVED. BUT THE REVOLT WAS A SIGN OF THE AMERICANS' FIERCE DESIRE FOR INDEPENDENCE FROM MEXICO.

THE MEXICAN WAR ENDED IN 1848. THE UNITED STATES HAD WON MUCH OF TODAY'S SOUTHWEST. IT ALSO NOW HAD THE VAST LANDS OF CALIFORNIA WITH ITS DESERTS AND LUSH VALLEYS. NO ONE KNEW WHAT OTHER RICHES THE LAND HELD . . .

WHEN THE STORY OF GOLD FIRST CAME OUT, MOST PEOPLE PAID LITTLE ATTENTION. SMALL AMOUNTS OF GOLD HAD BEEN FOUND BEFORE. BUT A BOLD MAN NAMED SAM BRANNAN SAW HIS CHANCE TO MAKE MONEY.

GENERAL S

GOLD! GOLD! GOLD!

SAM BRANNAN BOUGHT SHOVELS, PICKS, PANS, AND OTHER THINGS PEOPLE NEEDED TO FIND GOLD. HE OPENED A STORE NEAR THE AMERICAN RIVER. THEN HE RAN THROUGH THE STREETS OF SAN FRANCISCO WAVING A BOTTLE OF GOLD DUST. HE SHOUTED, "GOLD! GOLD! GOLD FROM THE AMERICAN RIVER!" HE STARTED "GOLD FEVER!"

ALMOST OVERNIGHT, CITIES AND TOWNS EMPTIED. PEOPLE RACED TO SUTTER'S MILL! HORSES WITH LOADED WAGONS CRASHED INTO EACH OTHER. MEN TRIED TO OUTRUN EACH OTHER. IN SAN FRANCISCO, THE NEWSPAPERS EVEN SHUT DOWN. THERE WAS NO ONE LEFT IN TOWN TO BUY THEM.

SAM BRANNON SAYS THERE'S GOLD IN THEM THERE HILLS!

GOLD SEEKERS PACKED PEACEFUL COLOMA VALLEY. THE SEARCH FOR GOLD BEGAN TO SPREAD NORTH AND SOUTH OF THE VALLEY. PEOPLE WERE FINDING GOLD EVERYWHERE. BY THE END OF 1848, 10,000 PEOPLE HAD COME TO CALIFORNIA LOOKING FOR GOLD!

BUT MANY AMERICANS IN THE EAST STILL DID NOT BELIEVE THE STORY. WHEN U.S. PRESIDENT JAMES K. POLK FINALLY SAID THAT THERE WAS GOLD IN CALIFORNIA, HIS WORDS MADE HEADLINES IN NEWSPAPERS EVERYWHERE. NOW, EVERYONE WANTED A PART OF THE TREASURE.

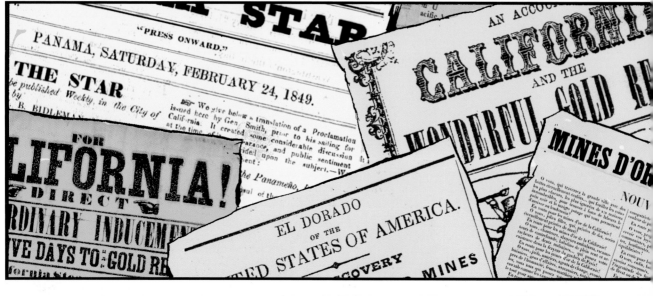

IN 1849, MOBS OF PEOPLE ARRIVED FROM AROUND THE WORLD. MOST PROSPECTORS, OR PEOPLE WHO DUG FOR GOLD, HAD NO IDEA WHAT TO EXPECT ON THE JOURNEY. FOR MOST PEOPLE, THE TRIP TO CALIFORNIA WAS VERY HARD.

MOST OF THE GOLD SEEKERS WALKED OR RODE A HORSE OR WAGON. TO GET TO CALIFORNIA, THEY HAD TO CROSS THE GREAT PLAINS, A HUGE PRAIRIE. THE TRIP TOOK ABOUT SIX MONTHS. MANY DIED OF THIRST OR DISEASE ON THE LONG JOURNEY.

OTHER PEOPLE TRAVELED BY SEA AROUND THE TIP OF SOUTH AMERICA. SOME SAILED TO PANAMA IN CENTRAL AMERICA, THEN HIKED THROUGH JUNGLES TO CATCH ANOTHER SHIP TO CALIFORNIA. THESE TRIPS COULD BE TERRIFYING. SHIPS WERE CROWDED AND FULL OF DISEASE. SOME SHIPS SANK IN HUGE STORMS ON THE WAY.

DESPITE THE DANGERS, PEOPLE KEPT FLOODING INTO CALIFORNIA. THE GOLD SEEKERS WHO CAME IN 1849 WERE KNOWN AS "FORTY-NINERS." ALL KINDS OF PEOPLE WORKED IN THE GOLD FIELDS. THEIR DAYS OF HARD WORK WERE LONG.

MORE THAN HALF THE WORKERS IN THE GOLD MINES WERE NATIVE AMERICAN. MOST NATIVE PEOPLE WERE FORCED TO WORK FOR NO PAY AS SLAVES IN THE MINES. SOME AFRICAN AMERICANS ALSO WORKED AS SLAVES. A FEW WERE ABLE TO BUY THEIR FREEDOM WITH GOLD. MOST, HOWEVER, GAINED NO REWARDS FROM THEIR LONG, HARD WORK.

A FEW WOMEN JOINED THE RUSH TO CALIFORNIA. WOMEN WERE ALLOWED TO RUN THEIR OWN BUSINESSES. FEWER COULD DO THIS BACK EAST. ONE WOMAN GOT RICH BY BAKING DOZENS OF PIES FOR HUNGRY WORKERS EACH DAY!

ONE OF THE LARGEST GROUPS OF MINERS CAME FROM CHINA. THE CHINESE ALSO WORKED HARD—FOR VERY LITTLE PAY.

THE GOLD RUSH YEARS

HUNDREDS OF MINING CAMPS SPROUTED NEAR SUTTER'S FORT. THESE CAMPS WERE NAMED FOR THE STRANGE AND SOMETIMES SCARY THINGS THAT HAPPENED THERE — GOUGE EYE, HANGTOWN, AND MAD MULE GULCH. SALOONS, LAUNDRIES, AND OTHER SMALL BUSINESSES WERE SET UP IN THESE TOWNS.

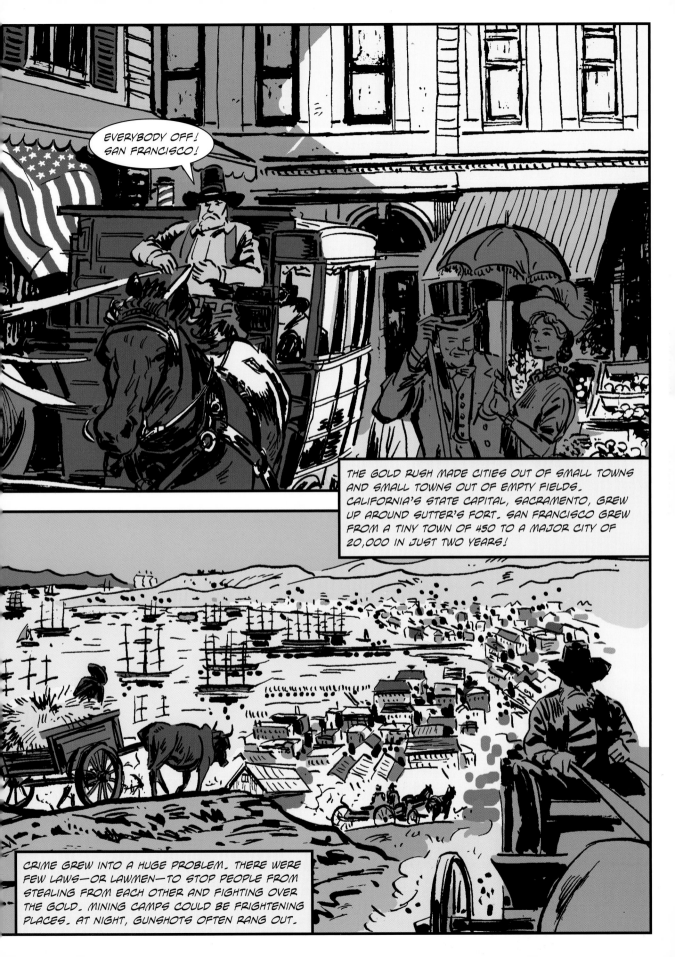

EVERYBODY OFF! SAN FRANCISCO!

THE GOLD RUSH MADE CITIES OUT OF SMALL TOWNS AND SMALL TOWNS OUT OF EMPTY FIELDS. CALIFORNIA'S STATE CAPITAL, SACRAMENTO, GREW UP AROUND SUTTER'S FORT. SAN FRANCISCO GREW FROM A TINY TOWN OF 450 TO A MAJOR CITY OF 20,000 IN JUST TWO YEARS!

CRIME GREW INTO A HUGE PROBLEM. THERE WERE FEW LAWS—OR LAWMEN—TO STOP PEOPLE FROM STEALING FROM EACH OTHER AND FIGHTING OVER THE GOLD. MINING CAMPS COULD BE FRIGHTENING PLACES. AT NIGHT, GUNSHOTS OFTEN RANG OUT.

LIFE WAS HARD FOR MOST OF THE FORTY-NINERS. THEY WORKED LONG HOURS EVERY DAY. MANY MINERS SPENT THEIR NIGHTS GAMBLING AND DRINKING IN SALOONS.

THERE WAS OFTEN NO CLEAN WATER OR DECENT FOOD IN THE CROWDED CAMPS. DIRTY LIVING CONDITIONS LED TO OUTBREAKS OF DISEASE, WHICH KILLED MANY. IN 1849 ALONE, 10,000 MINERS DIED OF ILLNESSES.

IN 1849, MINERS PANNING IN RIVERS OR DIGGING IN PITS FOUND GOLD WORTH NEARLY $40 MILLION ($1 BILLION TODAY).

WE'RE NOT FINDING ANYTHING HERE. LET'S MOVE UPRIVER!

BUT THE GOLD FIELDS WERE ALSO BECOMING CROWDED—AND THE GOLD WAS RUNNING OUT.

GETTING GOLD BY DIGGING MINES DEEP BENEATH THE SURFACE WAS EXPENSIVE AND DANGEROUS. MINERS HAD TO SPEND LONG DAYS CHIPPING AT ROCK IN DARK TUNNELS. SOMETIMES THE TUNNELS COLLAPSED.

EVENTUALLY, ONLY BIG COMPANIES COULD AFFORD TO DRILL FOR GOLD. DISAPPOINTED AND POOR, MANY FORTY-NINERS LEFT CALIFORNIA.

PEOPLE MADE MONEY IN MANY WAYS
DURING THE GOLD RUSH. THE CROWDED
MINING CAMPS OFTEN NEEDED FOOD
AND SUPPLIES. WATER WAS ESPECIALLY
IN SHORT SUPPLY.

SNAKE OIL

SNAKE OIL!
GUARANTEED TO CURE
WHAT AILS YA!

1 BOTTLE FOR $5

SOME PEOPLE TOOK ADVANTAGE OF THESE HARDSHIPS AND SHORTAGES. BUSINESSMEN
WERE ABLE TO SELL GOODS TO MINERS AT HIGH PRICES. ONE EGG COULD COST 50
CENTS—THAT'S $10 IN TODAY'S MONEY! A GLASS OF WATER COULD COST A THIRSTY MAN
$100! OTHERS EARNED MONEY IN MORE HONEST WAYS. DOCTORS AND DENTISTS CARED
FOR PEOPLE. BLACKSMITHS SHOD THEIR HORSES AND MULES.

KLANG
KLANG

EVEN ACTORS AND SINGERS MADE MONEY ENTERTAINING THE MINERS. MINERS MIGHT BE ENTERTAINED BY EVERYTHING FROM SQUARE DANCES TO PERFORMANCES OF PLAYS BY SHAKESPEARE.

BY 1854, THE CALIFORNIA GOLD RUSH WAS ENDING. AMERICANS BEGAN SEEKING GOLD AND SILVER IN OTHER PARTS OF THE WEST.

THE FIRST BIG STRIKE AFTER CALIFORNIA WAS IN COLORADO. IN 1858, BOTH GOLD AND SILVER WERE FOUND IN PIKE'S PEAK. OTHER DISCOVERIES WERE MADE IN NEVADA, ARIZONA, UTAH, AND MONTANA.

SIBERIA

ARCTIC OCEAN

BERING STRAIT

ALASKA

YUKON RIVER

UNEXPLORED DISTRICT

K L O N D I K E

★ DAWSON CITY

YUKON

JUNEAU

BRITISH COLUMBIA

BY THE 1890s THE SEARCH FOR GOLD HAD LED MINERS FARTHER AND FARTHER NORTH. THE LAST GREAT GOLD STRIKES WERE IN THE KLONDIKE REGION. THE KLONDIKE COVERED VAST AREAS OF WHAT ARE NOW ALASKA (IN THE U.S.) AND THE YUKON TERRITORY (IN CANADA). THE UNITED STATES HAD BOUGHT ALASKA FROM RUSSIA IN 1867. BUT IT WASN'T UNTIL THE KLONDIKE GOLD STRIKES THAT ANYONE PAID MUCH ATTENTION TO THIS BARREN LAND!

BAY

Gulf of Alaska

ALASKA PENINSULA

KODIAK ISLANDS

UNALASKA

PACIFIC OCEAN

THE SNOW AND FREEZING COLD WERE SO DIFFERENT FROM THE SEARING HEAT OF THE DESERT WHERE SO MUCH GOLD HAD BEEN FOUND.

DESPITE THE HARSH CLIMATE, LOTS OF PEOPLE CAME TO MINE IN ALASKA. THEY HAD TO TRAVEL OVER MILES AND MILES OF ICE AND SNOW. FEW FOUND THE RICHES THEY CAME FOR, HOWEVER.

AFTER MOST OF THE GOLD STRIKES IN THE WEST WERE USED UP, SETTLERS AND SOLDIERS BEGAN FORCING NATIVE AMERICANS TO LEAVE THEIR LAND. TO MAKE THE LIVES OF NATIVE PEOPLE EVEN WORSE, THE U.S. GOVERNMENT ALSO IGNORED TREATIES SIGNED WITH NATIVE TRIBES—AND NATIVE AMERICANS' RIGHTS TO THE LAND.

SADLY, MANY NATIVE PEOPLE LOST THEIR LIVES AT THE HANDS OF SOLDIERS CLEARING THE WAY FOR U.S. SETTLEMENTS. OTHERS WERE SENT TO LIVE ON RESERVATIONS SET UP BY THE UNITED STATES GOVERNMENT.

CALIFORNIA RAN OUT OF GOLD A LONG TIME AGO. BUT THE SPIRIT OF THE GOLD RUSH LIVES ON.

TODAY, CALIFORNIA IS ONE OF THE WEALTHIEST STATES IN THE UNION. IT IS HOME TO SOME OF THE MOST SUCCESSFUL BUSINESSES AND INDUSTRIES IN THE WORLD. BUT CALIFORNIA'S FORTUNES BEGAN WITH THE GOLD RUSH.

CALIFORNIA IS ALSO KNOWN FOR ITS CULTURAL MIX. ASIAN COMMUNITIES SPRANG UP DURING THE GOLD RUSH AND CONTINUE TODAY. THE LARGE LATINO POPULATION CAN BE TRACED TO EVEN OLDER SPANISH, MEXICAN, AND NATIVE ROOTS.

THE ONCE BUSY MINING CAMPS ARE QUIET NOW.
MANY WERE DESTROYED. BUT OTHERS, LIKE
BRANDY FLAT AND ROUGH AND READY, HAVE BEEN
PRESERVED AS "GHOST TOWNS."

TOURISTS FROM ALL OVER THE WORLD VISIT THESE HISTORIC TOWNS TO LEARN ABOUT THE GOLD RUSH. SOME PEOPLE EVEN SAY THAT MINERS HAUNT THE STREETS AT NIGHT STILL SEARCHING FOR THEIR GOLD!

MORE BOOKS TO READ

California. Seeds of a Nation (series). P. M. Boekhoff. (Kidhaven Press)

California Gold Rush. Landmark Events in American History (series). Michael V. Uschan (World Almanac Library)

California Gold Rush. Sheila Rivera. (ABDO Publishing Company)

Sightseers Guide to the California Gold Rush. Julie Ferris (Houghton Mifflin Company)

The New York Public Library Amazing Native American History: A Book of Answers for Kids. Liz Sonneborn (Wiley, John and Sons)

WEB SITES

California Gold Rush at Oakland Museum of California
www.museumca.org/goldrush.html

Gold Fever
www.pbs.org/wgbh/amex/gold/greetings.html

Gold Rush
www.calgoldrush.com/index.html

Gold Rush!
pbskids.org/wayback/goldrush/

Gold Rush Overview
www.parks.ca.gov/default.asp?page_id=1081

Please visit our web site at: www.worldalmanaclibrary.com
For a free color catalog describing World Almanac® Library's list of high-quality books and multimedia programs, call 1-800-848-2928 (USA) or 1-800-387-3178 (Canada). World Almanac® Library's fax: (414) 332-3567.

Library of Congress Cataloging-in-Publication Data

Hudson-Goff, Elizabeth.
  The California Gold Rush / Elizabeth Hudson-Goff and Michael V. Uschan.
    p. cm. — (Graphic histories)
  Includes bibliographical references.
  ISBN 0-8368-6202-3 (lib. bdg.)
  ISBN 0-8368-6254-6 (softcover)
  1. California—Gold discoveries—Juvenile literature. 2. California—History—1846-1850—Juvenile literature. 3. Frontier and pioneer life—California—Juvenile literature. I. Uschan, Michael V., 1948- II. Title. III. Series.
  F865.G64 2006
  979.4'04—dc22   2005027871

First published in 2006 by
World Almanac® Library
A Member of the WRC Media Family of Companies
330 West Olive Street, Suite 100
Milwaukee, WI 53212 USA

Copyright © 2006 by World Almanac® Library.

Produced by Design Press, a division of the Savannah College of Art and Design
Design: Janice Shay and Maria Angela Rojas
Editing: Kerri O'Hern and Elizabeth Hudson-Goff
Illustration: Guus Floor
World Almanac® Library editorial direction: Mark Sachner and Valerie J. Weber
World Almanac® Library art direction: Tammy West

Printed in the United States of America

1 2 3 4 5 6 7 8 9 10 09 08 07 06